A Visit to
CAMBODIA

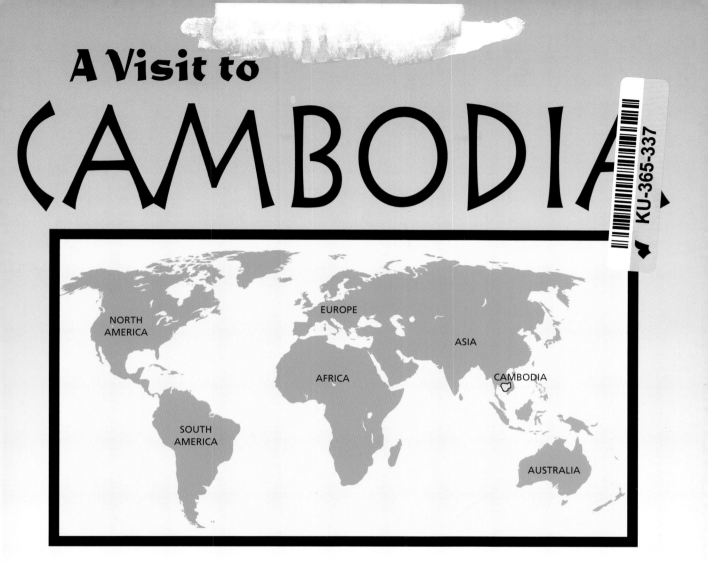

NORTH AMERICA

EUROPE

ASIA

AFRICA

CAMBODIA

SOUTH AMERICA

AUSTRALIA

Rob Alcraft

Heinemann
LIBRARY

First published in Great Britain by Heinemann Library,
Halley Court, Jordan Hill, Oxford OX2 8EJ,
a division of Reed Educational and Professional Publishing Ltd.

Heinemann is a registered trademark of Reed Educational & Professional Publishing Limited.

OXFORD   MELBOURNE   AUCKLAND
JOHANNESBURG   BLANTYRE   GABORONE
IBADAN   PORTSMOUTH (NH) USA   CHICAGO

Designed by AMR
Illustrations by Art Construction
Printed and bound in Hong Kong/China by South China Printing Co.

04 03 02 01 00
10 9 8 7 6 5 4 3 2 1

ISBN 0 431 08335 5

This title is also available in a hardback library edition (ISBN 0 431 08330 4).

British Library Cataloguing in Publication Data

Alcraft, Rob, 1966–
  A visit to Cambodia. – (Heinemann first library)
  1.Cambodia – Juvenile literature
  I.Title II.Cambodia
  959.6

Acknowledgements
The Publishers would like to thank the following for permission to reproduce photographs:
Colourific!: Michael Yamashita pp 13, 27, Catherine Karnow p 16; Hutchison Library: Sarah
Murray p 10, Nigel Sitwell pp 14, 28; Link: Sue Carpenter p 24, Jan Knapik p 26; Network: Roger
Hutchings p 19; Panos Pictures: Nic Dunlop pp 5, 21, Guiseppe Bizzarri p 7, Jim Holmes pp 8,
18, 22, Jon Spaull p 20, Irene Slegt p 23; Robert Harding Picture Library: Gavin Hellier p 25; Still
Pictures: Gilles Martin p 6; Telegraph Colour Library: Masterfile p 29; Trip: A Gasson pp 9, 17, B. A.
Dixie Dean p 11, Ask Images p 12, F Nichols p 15.

Cover photograph reproduced with permission of Robert Harding Picture Library.

Every effort has been made to contact copyright holders of any material reproduced in this
book. Any omissions will be rectified in subsequent printings if notice is given to the Publisher.

Any words appearing in bold, **like this**, are explained in the Glossary.

Contents

Cambodia

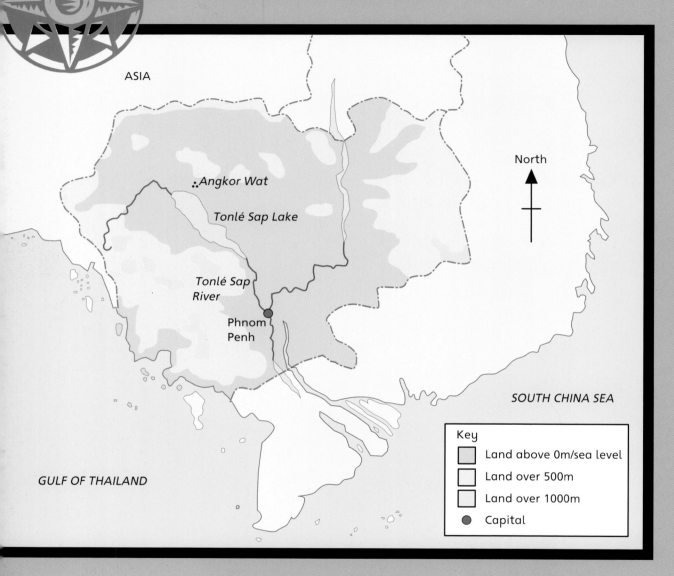

ASIA

Angkor Wat

Tonlé Sap Lake

Tonlé Sap River

Phnom Penh

North

SOUTH CHINA SEA

GULF OF THAILAND

Key
- Land above 0m/sea level
- Land over 500m
- Land over 1000m
- Capital

This is a map of Cambodia. Cambodia is in Asia.

It is always warm in Cambodia.
The land is quite flat and very green.

Land

Cambodia has thick forests. Tall trees can grow 50 metres high. There are elephants, leopards and bears.

In Cambodia, winds called the **monsoons** bring heavy rain. For four or five months it pours with rain every day. The rain makes the **crops** grow.

Landmarks

Angkor Wat is a 900 year old **temple**. It is built from blocks of stone that fit perfectly together. It was once part of a great city.

There is a huge lake in the middle of
Cambodia, called the Tonlé Sap lake.
It is wide and shallow, and full of fish.

Homes

Most people in Cambodia live in the countryside. They build their homes up on **stilts,** to keep them dry and cool. They make roofs from **palm tree** leaves.

There is one big city in Cambodia. It is
the **capital** city, called Phnom Penh. Here
families live in small flats and houses,
with one or two rooms.

Food

Cambodians eat with **chopsticks**. They eat lots of rice. Sometimes they add a sauce made of peanuts and fish, or a salad with herbs like garlic and mint.

Fish is a favourite Cambodian food. The fish is grilled and wrapped in little parcels of lettuce leaves and dipped in a spicy sauce.

Clothes

Cambodian clothes are light and cool. Men and women wear a cloth that they wrap around them like a skirt, or they wear trousers. On top they wear a shirt.

Some young Cambodian men become
Buddhist monks. They wear bright orange
robes and shave their heads. They must
keep 227 difficult promises to be a monk.

Work

When the **monsoon** rains come, farmers use **buffalo** to **plough** their fields. Then they plant their fields with rice. Each rice plant is pushed into the muddy fields by hand.

Cambodia does not have large factories
and industry. Many people work in
small shops repairing and making
things. Fishing is important too.

Transport

Most Cambodians are too poor to buy cars. Instead people use bicycles, motorcycles and special bicycle taxis.

For long journeys Cambodians take the bus, or go by boat. People travel by boat on the big rivers and on the huge Tonlé Sap lake.

Language

Cambodians speak a language called Khmer. Khmer writing goes from left to right, but there are no gaps between the words. Khmer has its own alphabet.

Khmer is very different from English.
There are 100 different words for rice.
There are two words for yes, one used
by women, and one used by men.

School

At school Cambodian children learn to read and write Khmer. They also learn English. The teacher is a very important person. The children take care to be good.

Not all young people can go to school. There has been war in Cambodia for more than 20 years. Lots of schools have been destroyed. Many teachers have been killed.

Free time

Cambodians love **festivals**. The whole family can put on their best clothes and visit their local **temple**.

Lots of Cambodian children help their parents in their free time. They help grow rice, or sell sweets and fruit to make money.

Celebrations

Cambodians celebrate the Khmer New Year in April. People give each other presents of new clothes, and take gifts to their local **temple**.

In the **monsoon** rains the big Tonlé Sap River gets so full, it flows backwards. When this happens, Cambodians have the Water **Festival**.

The Arts

Royal dance is a very old Cambodian art.
Dancers wear beautiful costumes. The
dances tell stories of love and battles.

In Cambodia there are many old **carvings**. Today artists still carve. They make beautiful images of the **Buddha**.

Factfile

Name	The Kingdom of Cambodia.
Capital	Cambodia's **capital** city is called Phnom Penh.
Language	Most Cambodians speak Khmer.
Population	There are 9.5 million people living in Cambodia.
Money	Cambodians use money called reil.
Religion	Most Cambodians are **Buddhists**.
Products	Cambodia produces rice, fish, rubber, paper and wood.

Words you can learn

joom reab suor (JEWM RE-a SUE-o)	hello
bat (BAH)	yes (said by men)
jas (JAHS)	yes (said by women)
te	no
ar kun (R KUN)	thank you
suom (SUE-um)	please
pee	two
bram	five
bram-pee	seven

Glossary

Buddhist	Buddhism is a religion. Buddhists believe that if they live a good life, then they will be rewarded
Buddha	was a man who lived long ago. Buddhists follow his teachings
buffalo	a large animal that looks a bit like a cow. Buffalos are often used in Asia instead of tractors
capital	a capital city is a country's most important city. It is where the government lives
carvings	pictures made in stone or wood
chopsticks	a pair of sticks held in one hand, used to lift food to the mouth
crops	plants, such as rice, that are grown for food
festivals	are like parties, but a whole town or country joins in
monk	young men, and sometimes women, who spend time learning about a religion like Buddhism
monsoon	a name for a season with lots of rain
palm tree	a tree that has a long thin trunk, with a tuft of leaves right at the top
plough	this is the name for the job of breaking up the soil before seeds are planted
stilts	supports, like legs
temple	a special place for **Buddhists**, like a church or mosque

Index